SNAKES SET I

BOA CONSTRICTORS

Megan M. Gunderson
ABDO Publishing Company

visit us at
www.abdopublishing.com

Published by ABDO Publishing Company, 8000 West 78th Street, Edina, Minnesota 55439. Copyright © 2011 by Abdo Consulting Group, Inc. International copyrights reserved in all countries. No part of this book may be reproduced in any form without written permission from the publisher. The Checkerboard Library™ is a trademark and logo of ABDO Publishing Company.

Printed in the United States of America, North Mankato, Minnesota.
042010
092010

 PRINTED ON RECYCLED PAPER

Cover Photo: Photo Researchers
Interior Photos: Getty Images pp. 6–7; Peter Arnold pp. 5, 9, 12, 14–15, 18–19; Photo Researchers p. 17; Photolibrary pp. 11, 21

Editor: BreAnn Rumsch
Art Direction & Cover Design: Neil Klinepier

Library of Congress Cataloging-in-Publication Data

Gunderson, Megan M., 1981-
  Boa constrictors / Megan M. Gunderson.
     p. cm. -- (Snakes)
  Includes index.
  ISBN 978-1-61613-433-4
  1. Boa constrictor--Juvenile literature. I. Title.
  QL666.O63G86 2011
   597.96'7--dc22
                                    2010011143

CONTENTS

BOA CONSTRICTORS

Boa constrictors are some of the world's most well-known reptiles. Like all snakes, these stunning creatures are vertebrates. They have long, slithering bodies and tails.

Snakes are cold-blooded creatures. That simply means their surroundings affect their body temperature. In order to survive, snakes must not get too hot or too cold. So, they lie in the sun to warm up or find shade to cool down.

Boa constrictors belong to the family **Boidae**. Their common name is the same as their scientific name, *boa constrictor*. Scientists have identified many boa constrictor **subspecies**. These carnivores are named for the way they kill their food. They coil around their prey and squeeze it to death!

Boa constrictors are also called common boas.

SIZES

The word *boa* is Latin for "a large serpent." Boa constrictors can weigh more than 100 pounds (45 kg)! Their heads look small compared to their big, heavy bodies.

A boa constrictor's length depends on its **subspecies**. From nose to tail, some grow more than 16 feet (5 m) in length. Yet, most are not longer than 11 feet (3.3 m). Hog Island boa constrictors measure just 3 feet (1 m) long.

A boa constrictor's strong, muscular body helps it kill prey and climb trees.

COLORS

Stretchy skin and dry scales cover a snake's long body. On boa constrictors, the scales form special color patterns. These patterns help boa constrictors blend in with their surroundings.

Boa constrictors have a range of colors. They can be cream, tan, silver, or gray. Some boa **subspecies** are darker or lighter than others. For example, the Argentine boa can have a black base color. The Hog Island boa is more pastel.

All boas are covered with blotches. These saddle-shaped markings are often dark brown or red. They may be outlined in black.

Some boa constrictors have red tails.

WHERE THEY LIVE

Do you picture boa constrictors living in the jungle? Many people do. But actually, boa constrictors live in a wide variety of **habitats**.

Some boa constrictors do live in rain forests and on tropical islands. But they are found in **grasslands** and semidesert areas, too. They also live by plantations, agricultural land, and other areas near humans. Boa constrictors can also swim. These snakes are often found near rivers.

Whatever their habitat, boa constrictors usually live on the ground. They hide out in fallen logs as well as burrows made by other animals. Yet they are good climbers. So, those that live in forests may spend time in trees.

Young boas are more likely than older boas to climb trees.

WHERE THEY ARE FOUND

Boa constrictors are huge snakes with a wide range! They live from Mexico, through Central America, to South America. Many islands provide homes to boa constrictors. These include Trinidad, Tobago, Dominica, St. Lucia, and Saboga Island.

Different areas feature specific boa constrictor **subspecies**. The Argentine boa is found farther south than any other type of boa. It lives in Paraguay and northern Argentina. The Peruvian boa makes its home in just one small area of northwestern Peru.

The Hog Island boa lives off the coast of Honduras.

NORTH
AMERICA

Gulf of Mexico

Atlantic Ocean

Pacific Ocean

N

SOUTH
AMERICA

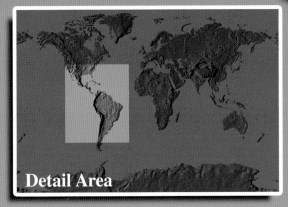

Detail Area

Where Boa Constrictors Live

SENSES

Day and night, boa constrictors use their keen senses to survive. They use their eyes to check out their surroundings. Snakes most easily spot things that are moving.

A boa constrictor's tongue isn't just for tasting. It is also an important part of smelling! A snake flicks out its forked tongue to pick up odors in the air. Back inside the mouth, the Jacobson's **organ** identifies these scents. It passes that information on to the brain.

Snakes do not have **external** ears. But, they have a sense of

Instead of movable eyelids, scales protect a snake's eyes.

hearing. Their jawbones pick up vibrations in the ground. These travel through bones in the head to the snake's inner ears. From there, they travel to the brain to be analyzed.

DEFENSE

A boa constrictor's coloring is important to its survival. Camouflage helps it avoid natural predators. Hidden in its surroundings, a boa constrictor is safe.

What if an enemy finds a boa constrictor? The snake can try to slither away to safety. If escape isn't an option, the boa will become **aggressive**. Boa constrictors coil up, make loud hissing noises, and bite! Their sharp teeth make bites painful, but boas do not release **venom**.

Large boa constrictors have few natural enemies. Young boas face danger from birds, raccoonlike coatis, and other animals.

A boa constrictor's color pattern makes it difficult to spot in its natural habitat.

Humans are the boa constrictor's greatest enemy. People capture boas to sell them as pets. They sell their skins, too. **Habitat** destruction also threatens the boa constrictor's survival.

FOOD

Camouflage doesn't just protect boa constrictors from their enemies. It also hides them from their prey. Boa constrictors lie still until prey wanders close by. Then, they strike out and grab on with their sharp teeth.

Since boas are constrictors, they wrap around the prey they catch. Then, they squeeze until the animal can no longer breathe. Once the prey dies, boa constrictors swallow it whole! Usually, they eat prey headfirst.

Hungry boa constrictors will feast on nearly any animal they can swallow. They will snack on birds and lizards. Boa constrictors also eat a variety of mammals, including coatis, deer, tree porcupines, and dogs. These hungry snakes catch bats by hanging from trees or cave mouths. They grab their prey right out of the air!

Boa constrictors help control
populations of rodents and other pests.

BABIES

After mating, a female boa constrictor may become **pregnant**. She carries her young for five to eight months. Then, she gives birth to 10 to 64 live babies. This number depends partly on the mother's size. Larger females are able to carry more babies at once.

Newborn boa constrictors are about 20 inches (50 cm) long. Soon after birth, baby boas **shed** for the first time. Young snakes continue to shed whenever they outgrow their skin. Snakes also shed if their skin becomes injured or worn.

Snakes never stop growing. So, adults continue to shed as long as they live. In **captivity**, boa constrictors have survived for 25 to 35 years.

A snake's skin usually peels off in one big piece!

GLOSSARY

aggressive (uh-GREH-sihv) - displaying hostility.

Boidae (BOH-uh-dee) - the scientific name for the boa family. This family includes boa constrictors and anacondas.

captivity - the state of being captured and held against one's will.

external - of, relating to, or being on the outside.

grassland - land on which the main plants are grasses.

habitat - a place where a living thing is naturally found.

organ - a part of an animal or a plant composed of several kinds of tissues. An organ performs a specific function. The heart, liver, gallbladder, and intestines are organs of an animal.

pregnant - having one or more babies growing within the body.

shed - to cast off hair, feathers, skin, or other coverings or parts by a natural process.

subspecies - a group of related organisms ranking below a species. Members of a subspecies often share a common geographic range.

venom - a poison produced by some animals and insects. It usually enters a victim through a bite or a sting.

WEB SITES

To learn more about boa constrictors, visit ABDO Publishing Company on the World Wide Web at **www.abdopublishing.com**. Web sites about boa constrictors are featured on our Book Links page. These links are routinely monitored and updated to provide the most current information available.

INDEX